MORE

Improve your sight-reading!

A workbook for examinations

PIANO

Grade 2

PAUL HARRIS

FABER *ff* MUSIC

INTRODUCTION

Welcome to *More Improve your sight-reading!*, the perfect follow-up to *Improve your sight-reading!*

Good sight-reading is all about getting into good habits. By working through this book carefully, you'll develop these habits and begin to sight-read fluently, accurately and confidently.

Using the workbook

1. Rhythmic exercises These begin from Stage 2. Make sure you have grasped the rhythms fully before you go on to the melodic exercises: it is vital that you really know how the rhythms work. There are a number of ways to do the exercises: perhaps tapping the pulse with one foot while you clap the rhythm, or the other way round; tapping the pulse with one hand and the rhythm with the other, and so on. Experiment!

2. Melodic exercises These exercises are based on the concept stated for the Stage, and also give some help with fingering. If you want to sight-read fluently and accurately, get into the simple habit of working through each exercise in the following way before you begin to play it:

- Make sure that you understand the rhythm and counting. Clap the exercise through.

- Know what notes you are going to play and what fingering you are going to use.

- Try as best you can to *hear the piece through in your head*. Always play the first note to help.

3. Prepared pieces Work your way through the questions first, as these will help you to think about or 'prepare' the piece. Don't begin playing until you are pretty sure you know *exactly* how the piece goes.

4. Unprepared pieces This doesn't mean you shouldn't prepare them! Instead, it is now up to you to discover the clues to each piece. Give yourself about a minute and do your best to 'understand' the piece before you play. Check the rhythms and hand position, and try to hear the piece in your head.

Always remember to feel the pulse and to keep going steadily once you've begun.

Good luck and happy sight-reading!

© 2005 by Faber Music Ltd
First published in 2005 by Faber Music Ltd
3 Queen Square London WC1N 3AU
Music processed by Silverfen
Printed in England by Caligraving Ltd.
All rights reserved

ISBN 0-571-52394-3

To buy Faber Music publications or to find out about the full range of titles available
please contact your local music retailer or Faber Music sales enquiries:

Faber Music Limited, Burnt Mill, Elizabeth Way, Harlow, CM20 2HX England
Tel: +44 (0)1279 82 89 82 Fax: +44 (0)1279 82 89 83
sales@fabermusic.com   fabermusic.com

STAGE 1

Reading right and left hands together is no more difficult than reading just one hand at a time!

The	on	then	and
cat	the	saw a	had a
sat	mat	rat	chat!

No problem with that!

Remember: the most important thing is the way you prepare each piece before you begin playing it.

So, before you start to play, look carefully through the music and:

- check that you understand the rhythm and counting

- know what notes you are going to play and work out the fingering

- try to have a good idea of what it's going to sound like.

MELODIC EXERCISES
Remember to count two bars in before you begin – one bar out loud and one bar in your head.

This music is copyright. Photocopying is illegal.

PREPARED PIECES

1 In which key is this piece?

2 Play the scale and arpeggio, right hand and then left hand.

3 Are there any scale or arpeggio patterns?

4 Can you spot any repeated patterns?

5 What are the first notes of each hand?

6 Play the first notes of each hand and then hear the piece through as best you can before you begin.

1 To what pattern do the first four notes belong?

2 Are the first four bars and the second four bars similar in any ways?

3 Are there any scale patterns?

4 Clap the rhythm of the first four bars of the right hand following the music and then from memory.

5 Tap the rhythm of the piece (both hands) on a table top or the piano lid.

6 Play the first notes of each hand and then hear the piece through as best you can before you begin.

UNPREPARED PIECES

STAGE 2

RHYTHMIC EXERCISES

Don't forget to count in two bars before you begin each exercise – one bar out loud and one bar silently.

MELODIC EXERCISES

Try to hear each piece in your head before you play it.

PREPARED PIECES

1   In which key is this piece?

2   Play the scale and arpeggio.

3   Tap the rhythms of both hands together, whilst counting the pulse out loud.

4   Can you spot any repeated patterns?

5   What are the first notes of each part?

6   Play the first note of each hand and then hear the piece through as best you can, before you begin.

Boldly

1   In which key is this piece?

2   Play the scale and arpeggio.

3   Are there any scale or arpeggio patterns?

4   What is the similarity between bar 1 of the right hand and bar 2 of the left hand?

5   Tap the rhythm (both hands) on a table top or the piano lid and count out loud.

6   Play the first note of each hand and then hear the piece through as best you can, before you begin.

Smoothly

UNPREPARED PIECES

STAGE 3

$\frac{3}{8}$

RHYTHMIC EXERCISES

In $\frac{3}{8}$ time, a quaver (or eighth note) is equal to one beat. Count three quavers in a bar.

MELODIC EXERCISES

Look out for repeated patterns. Try to hear each piece in your head before you play it.

PREPARED PIECES

1 How will you count this piece?

2 Counting out loud, tap the rhythm of both hands on a table top or the piano lid.

3 Tapping the pulse, hear the rhythm of the right hand in your head.

4 How many repeated patterns can you spot?

5 Look at the first two bars for a few moments, then play them from memory.

6 Play the first note of each hand, then try to hear the whole piece in your head.

Allegretto

1 What is the key of the piece?

2 To what pattern do the first three notes belong?

3 Are there any F sharps?

4 Is the pattern of the first two bars repeated?

5 Is this a serious or a humorous piece?

6 Play the first note and then, clapping the pulse, hear the piece in your head as best you can.

With spirit

UNPREPARED PIECES

STAGE 4

RHYTHMIC EXERCISES

Don't forget to count in two bars before you begin each exercise – one bar out loud and one bar silently.

MELODIC EXERCISES

Think carefully about the key of each piece before you begin. Get into the habit of playing the scale.

PREPARED PIECES

1 In which key is this piece?

2 Play the scale and arpeggio.

3 Can you find any scale patterns in this piece?

4 Tap the rhythm of both hands of the piece, counting out loud.

5 Look at the first two bars for a few moments, then play them from memory.

6 Play the first note of each hand and then try to hear the whole piece in your head.

Flowing

1 Play the scale and arpeggio of the key of this piece.

2 What do you notice about the first four bars?

3 What is the character of this piece? How will you express it?

4 Where will you have to change hand position?

5 In your head, hear the rhythm of each hand separately, then hear the rhythms of the two hands together.

6 Play the first note and then, clapping the pulse, hear the piece in your head as best you can.

Spiritoso

UNPREPARED PIECES

STAGE 5

E minor

RHYTHMIC EXERCISES

Sometimes count in four bars before you begin each exercise – two bars out loud and two bars silently.

MELODIC EXERCISES

PREPARED PIECES

1   In which key is this piece?

2   Play the scale and arpeggio, right hand and then left hand.

3   Can you find any repeated patterns in this piece?

4   Count out loud and clap the rhythm of the right hand.

5   Now tap the rhythm of both hands together.

6   Look at the first two bars for a few moments, then play them from memory.

Andante

1   To what chord do the first two notes of the right hand belong?

2   Where will you have to change hand position?

3   Clap the rhythm of the left hand, whilst counting the beats out loud.

4   What do you notice about the first three bars?

5   Play the first three bars of the right hand – now try to hear those same bars in your head.

6   Play the first left-hand note, then try to hear the whole piece in your head as best you can.

Heavily

UNPREPARED PIECES

STAGE 6

A major

RHYTHMIC EXERCISES

Don't forget to count yourself in before you begin each exercise.

MELODIC EXERCISES

PREPARED PIECES

1 In which key is this piece? Play the scale and arpeggio, right hand and then left hand.

2 Does the opening music return?

3 Tap the rhythm of both hands on a table top or the piano lid.

4 Does either hand move position during the piece?

5 Study the first two bars of the right hand for a few moments, then play them from memory.

6 Play the first note and then, clapping the pulse, hear the piece in your head as best you can.

1 Does either hand change position during this piece?

2 Can you spot any passages based on scale patterns?

3 Are there any repeated patterns?

4 Clap the left-hand line and *think* the right hand silently.

5 What does **Con spirito** mean? What effect will it have on your performance?

6 Play the first note of each hand and then try to hear the piece in your head as best you can.

UNPREPARED PIECES

STAGE 7

Always remember these golden rules, and your sight-reading will go from strength to strength:

- Don't begin playing until you are fairly sure that you will get the piece right.
- Once you begin **keep the pulse steady** and **don't stop**.

Check:

- that you know how the rhythms go
- your hand position
- that you've tried to hear it through in your head before you begin.

MELODIC EXERCISES

Remember to count at least two bars before you begin each exercise – one out loud and one silently.

PREPARED PIECES

1 In which key is this piece? Play the scale and arpeggio.

2 Compare the first and second bars of the right hand.

3 Study the first two bars of the right hand for a few moments – now play them from memory.

4 Now look at the first two bars of the left hand. Play bars 1 and 2 (both hands) from memory.

5 Are there any scale patterns in this piece?

6 Clapping the pulse, hear the piece in your head as best you can.

1 In which key is this piece? Play the scale and arpeggio.

2 Does the rhythm of the left-hand first two bars return? Hear the rhythm in your head then clap it.

3 Does the melodic shape of the left-hand first two bars return?

4 Study the first two bars of the right-hand part (bars 2 and 3) for a few moments
   – now play them from memory.

5 What is the character of this piece?

6 Clapping the pulse, hear the piece in your head as best you can.

UNPREPARED PIECES

Improve your scales!

Paul Harris's brilliant series of workbooks uses 'finger fitness' exercises, scale and arpeggio 'key' studies and pieces, and simple improvisations to help you to play scales and arpeggios with real confidence, as well as promoting a solid basis for the learning of repertoire and for sight-reading. An invaluable resource for students, *Improve your scales!* covers all the keys and ranges required for the Associated Board syllabus, helping you to pick up those valuable extra marks in exams.

Improve your scales! Grade 1	0-571-51548-7
Improve your scales! Grade 2	0-571-51549-5
Improve your scales! Grade 3	0-571-51550-9
Improve your scales! Grade 4	0-571-51599-1
Improve your scales! Grade 5	0-571-52132-0

Improve your practice!

You've probably heard the expression 'practice makes perfect'. But it's not just the quantity of practice that's important; it's the quality. With the aid of *Improve your practice!*, you will begin to develop ways of making the most out of your practice. What's more, you'll also find that your wider musical skills of aural, theory, sight-reading, improvisation and composition develop alongside. *Improve your practice!* is the essential companion for pianists, encapsulating Paul Harris's failsafe approach to learning.

Piano Grade 1	ISBN 0-571-52261-0
Piano Grade 2	ISBN 0-571-52262-9
Piano Grade 3	ISBN 0-571-52263-7
Piano Grade 4	ISBN 0-571-52264-5
Piano Grade 5	ISBN 0-571-52265-3

FABER *ff* MUSIC